CONQUERING BINGE EATING

CONQUERING BINGE EATING

NITA MALLICK AND STEPHANIE WATSON

ROSEN
PUBLISHING®

New York

Published in 2016 by The Rosen Publishing Group, Inc.
29 East 21st Street, New York, NY 10010

Copyright © 2016 by The Rosen Publishing Group, Inc.

First Edition

Library of Congress Cataloging in Publication Data

Mallick, Nita.
 Conquering binge eating / Nita Mallick and Stephanie Watson. – First edition.
     pages cm. – (Conquering eating disorders)
 Includes bibliographical references and index.
 ISBN 978-1-4994-6199-2 (library bound)
 1. Eating disorders in adolescence–Juvenile literature. 2. Eating disorders
 –Treatment–Juvenile literature. I. Watson, Stephanie, 1969- II. Title.
 RC552.E18M358 2016
 616.85'2600835–dc23
                                                                2015019912

For many of the images in this book, the people photographed are models.
The depictions do not imply actual situations or events.

Manufactured in the United States of America

CONTENTS

Identifying Binge Eating Disorder

Achieving a healthy relationship with food can be tricky even for the most health conscious individuals. However, when a relationship with food becomes so unhealthy that it interferes with basic daily functioning, it is likely an eating disorder—a potentially life-threatening medical illness. Eating disorders have both a physical and emotional component. Millions of people are or have been affected by an eating disorder in their lifetime.

There are different kinds of eating disorders. They can involve a dangerously low intake of food, a dangerously high intake, or other abnormal eating habits. The three major types are anorexia nervosa, bulimia nervosa, and binge eating disorder. The most common among adults is binge eating disorder, according to the National Institute of Diabetes and Digestive and Kidney Diseases. The Institute estimates that 3.5 percent of adult women, 2 percent of adult men, and 1.6 percent of adolescents have it. Binge eating disorder—characterized by consuming large amounts of food frequently and feeling unable to stop—often results in obesity, which, in turn, can lead to major health risks including diabetes, high blood pressure, and heart disease. However, with the proper treatment and support, many have overcome binge eating disorder to develop a healthy relationship with food and with themselves.

Binge eating disorder, also known as compulsive overeating, affects about four million Americans, according to the US Department of Health and Human Services.

People who eat a lot of food in a short amount of time, and do so often, are at high risk of being obese. According to some estimates, two people out of three who have binge eating disorder are obese.

The Basics

Binge eating disorder, also known as compulsive overeating, is different from occasional bingeing—eating a large amount of food once in a while, such as on holidays or special occasions. People with binge eating disorder regularly—at least once a week—consume much more food than their bodies can use and don't stop even when they feel full. Unlike people with bulimia, people with binge eating disorder do not get rid of the food, or purge, after they have eaten. Binge eating usually results in weight gain and, often, obesity.

Although some distinguish between binge eating and food addiction, the two conditions are often related. Much in the way that alcoholics are addicted to alcohol, binge eaters are addicted to, or hooked on, food. Their lives are controlled by thoughts of what, when, and how much they will eat. They feel so guilty about their lack of self-control about food that they often eat alone or hide their food and eat it secretly. They eat whether or not they are hungry. They often eat large amounts of sweets and high-calorie foods and do not stop until they feel uncomfortably full. These episodes are usually followed by feelings of shame, disgust, sadness, or other negative emotions.

Binge eaters generally enjoy eating sweets such as cupcakes and other sugary desserts and high-calorie meals. They stop eating only when they feel unbearably full.

What Makes It an Eating Disorder?

As with binge eating disorder, other eating disorders involve some kind of extreme emotional reaction to food. The two best-known eating disorders are anorexia nervosa and bulimia nervosa. Anorexia is a condition in which a person believes he or she is overweight and refuses to eat—in order to lose excessive amounts of weight. Bulimia is when a person binges, or eats large amounts of food in a short period of time, and then purges, or gets rid of all the food by self-induced vomiting, abuse of laxatives, diet pills and/or diuretics, or fasting.

Compulsive exercise (also sometimes called exercise addiction) is also considered a serious eating disorder–related problem. This conduct is when a person constantly exercises to get rid of calories. This behavior is also known as exercise bulimia, because the person is using exercise to purge food from the body.

The cause of eating disorders remains unknown. There are often social or environmental factors that might trigger an eating disorder and possibly a genetic or biological basis as well. Depression or anxiety might also increase the risk of developing an eating disorder. While any or all of these might play a role, there does not seem to be a sole cause.

Who Does Binge Eating Disorder Affect?

Most teenage girls and many teenage boys have probably been unhappy with their body once in a while. It is nearly impossible to live in a culture obsessed with fitness and thinness without having a negative body image at least occasionally. However, teens who suffer from binge eating are never free of these bad feelings.

Binge eating disorder is the most common of all eating disorders. According to a 2011 study, 1.6 percent of teens out of ten thousand surveyed were affected by binge eating disorder, compared to 0.3 percent affected by anorexia and 0.9 percent by bulimia. Both males and females can be affected. Of the adults affected by binge eating disorder, about 40 percent are male and 60 percent are female.

Behavioral and Emotional Signs of Binge Eating

Most people overeat now and then, and that's typical. But if you often eat until you are overstuffed or you eat large amounts of food when you are not really hungry or it's not a regular mealtime, you may be a binge eater.

A binge eating disorder left untreated can lead to serious health problems, as well as psychological problems. It is important to determine as early as possible whether you have a problem. The earlier you identify the problem, the sooner you can get treatment. There are numerous behavioral and emotional indicators of binge eating disorder. The following are some of the most common signs.

Consuming Food Even When You're Full

Experts note that there are two types of hunger: physical and emotional. Physical hunger is the slight discomfort or burning feeling you get in your stomach when it is empty and in need of food. This is a natural and healthy signal that lets you know when it's time to eat. Emotional hunger, on the other hand, has little to do with the body's physical needs. When people experience emotional hunger, they eat to try to fill an emptiness they feel in their hearts and minds.

Because binge eaters have learned to eat in response to their emotional needs instead of their physical needs, they often reach a point at which they are no longer able to experience and recognize real hunger. With the messages between the brain and the stomach short-circuited, binge eaters continue to eat even after eating too much. Overeating often leads to weight gain, and weight gain usually leads to more of the same painful feelings that caused the person to turn to food in the first place.

Consuming Large Amounts of Food

Binge eaters often turn to food as a way to cope. They consume large volumes of food in a relatively short period—around two hours or so. They usually eat quickly and consume a large quantity of high-calorie foods. Bingeing episodes occur regularly—at least once a week and often more. These episodes frequently accompany feelings of extreme emotions, such as anger or fear.

For binge eaters, these episodes reflect a compulsion. They feel powerless to stop or control what they are doing.

Hiding Food

Secretive snackers eat late at night or hide food away and eat it when no one is looking. They may eat just a little bit at a time so that their family and friends don't notice the missing food. Some may eat normally around others and then binge when alone. They hide their eating because they are too ashamed to let other people see what they are doing. Eating secretly also makes them feel more powerful and in control over at least one aspect of their lives.

Some people who binge eat do so at uncommon times, such as late at night. They can eat normally when they are with people but then they gorge themselves uncontrollably when they are alone.

Eating Frequently Throughout the Day

Someone who grazes eats constantly—snacking on candy bars between classes, munching cookies in the locker room, or eating at home while talking to friends on the phone. Male athletes often graze when trying to bulk up in order to make a sports team. Other boys may cheer them on, encouraging the grazing behavior.

People who graze don't act as though they are ashamed of overeating, because they do it in front of people. But inside, they don't feel good about what they're doing. They often suffer from low self-esteem and use food to gain attention and acceptance.

Dieting Frequently

Binge eaters often go on and off diets, repeatedly losing and gaining back large amounts of weight. Binge eating may even begin after a major diet. Many times, binge eaters may experience no weight loss after dieting. They may try crash diets, diet pills, or other diet trends. However, these are often ineffective.

Part of the problem is that diets do not address the psychological component of binge eating disorder. Another factor is that the hunger caused by a strict diet may prompt food cravings or an impulse to overeat.

Negative Feelings

Binge eaters are often plagued by negative emotions. Many experience feelings of shame and guilt—disgust for their bodies or eating habits or guilt about viewing eating as one of their only pleasures in life. Many judge themselves as "good" or "bad" according to the foods they eat or the size they are. Many binge eaters also feel a

Binge eaters also secretly hoard, or stockpile, food or hide it so that they can eat it later. This is sometimes called closet eating, and those who do so often feel embarrassed by how much they are overeating, so they eat alone.

lack of self-control over their eating. Some become sad, upset, or even depressed. They may avoid friends or family out of embarrassment over their binge eating. Eating alone or hiding food is another common response.

Binge eating is something people may do in response to a problem, such as a parent's alcoholism or stress at school. Because they can't talk about their problems with their friends or deal with them alone, they use bingeing as a way to escape the fear, tension, stress, or anger they feel. All they can think about is eating.

The relief that binge eaters feel while bingeing is only temporary, though, and many may not experience any satisfaction, regardless of how much they consume. Afterward, they may feel guilty about what they have eaten. They eventually criticize and blame themselves. It can be a vicious cycle in which binge eaters turn back to food to relieve their feelings of guilt or shame. And, unfortunately, when they stop eating, their stressful situation hasn't gone away.

MYTHS and *FACTS*

MYTH If I'm overweight or obese, I must have binge eating disorder.

Many binge eaters do become overweight or obese; however, most people who are obese are not binge eaters. Obesity is a medical illness that can be the result of a variety of factors, not just binge eating. Binge eating disorder has a psychological component, while obesity alone does not.

MYTH All binge eaters are overweight or obese.

You cannot tell if a person is a binge eater or not just by looking at him or her. Although weight gain is likely with binge eating disorder, people of normal weight can still be binge eaters and exhibit the behavioral and emotional signs associated with binge eating disorder.

MYTH I binge eat healthy food, so I don't really have a problem.

High-calorie foods are a common choice for binge eaters, but bingeing on any food, whether it's considered "healthy" or "unhealthy," can lead to major health risks and needs to be addressed. When consumed in an unhealthy way, no food is healthy.

MYTH Binge eating only affects young girls and women.

Binge eating affects people of all ages, male and female. It can begin at any stage of life.

MYTH If I have binge eating disorder, I will never be able to feel control over my eating.

All eating disorders are treatable, including binge eating disorder. Various combinations of medical, behavioral, and psychological therapies can help address the issues underlying binge eating. Former binge eaters can go on to achieve a healthy relationship with food and a sense of control over what they eat.

CHAPTER TWO

Roots of the Problem

It is important to remember that having binge eating disorder does not mean you are lazy or undisciplined. There are a variety of factors that may dispose someone to become affected by binge eating disorder. It is an illness that has many possible social, psychological, and biological causes. Understanding the roots of binge eating disorder requires examining how society can affect your relationship with food, your body, and your mind.

The Body and Society

Do you sometimes wake up in the morning, look in the mirror, and say, "I feel fat today"? But how can you *feel* fat? Fat is not a feeling, like happiness, sadness, excitement, or fear. When you say, "I feel fat," you are not really talking about the size of your body. You are talking about a thought ("I think I'm fat") that often describes deeper feelings of unworthiness or shame.

It is easy to see why people become dissatisfied with their bodies when they experience problems. We live in a culture that teaches us that we should never be happy with the size and shape of our bodies. Everywhere we look—on the Internet, in the movies, on television, in magazines and newspapers, on billboards and other advertisements—we get the message that fat is bad and unhealthy while thin is beautiful and healthy.

Pop Culture

Ask a group of people to describe the ideal body and you'll probably hear a variety of answers: the name of a famous model or celebrity, a set of measurements, or a description of the size and shape of certain body parts. One answer you will surely never hear, not even from models and movie stars, is, "The ideal body is my body." Nearly everyone who believes that there is an ideal body describes it as thinner, stronger, healthier, and better than his or her own. The ideal body is always something that everyone lacks, something no one can ever achieve—not with diets, pills, or even plastic surgery. In other words, the ideal body is always impossible to attain because people rarely allow themselves to believe that their own bodies are good enough.

Pop culture is full of contradictory and damaging messages about body image. The fashion sections of magazines for girls and women show ultrathin models wearing the latest styles, leading many teens to feel self-conscious of their own bodies. Then the health and fitness sections of the same magazines seem to offer help by promising a thinner, smaller body after just a few weeks on some fad diet. But the

Today, numerous fashion industry officials have banned unhealthy weights in models to combat eating disorders and the idealization of thinness.

slimness featured in magazines is impossible for most people to achieve. People come in a variety of shapes and sizes, and each type of body has its own beauty. It's easy to forget that the slim figures featured in magazines are just one type of body shape.

People Around You

The myth of the ideal body can be particularly troubling for teens because the teenage years are full of difficult physical, emotional, and social changes. Puberty can be especially difficult for girls because their bodies naturally put on more weight to prepare for menstruation. Many teens feel that they will not be popular if they have the "wrong" body shape, and classmates and schoolmates may make matters worse by encouraging that kind of thinking. But many teens are unaware that genes play a big part in determining their body shapes. Teens with bodies that don't fit naturally into the current ideal often fear that they will never be attractive to anyone. Well-meaning friends and family sometimes make these insecurities worse by suggesting dangerous solutions, such as fad diets and diet pills.

The real solution is to learn to love and accept yourself—no matter what your body size or shape—and find healthier ways to deal with food and feelings.

Food and Society

When you describe your favorite food, do you say you "love" it? Most people do. Eating food can be a very sensual experience. Your sense of taste is involved, of course, but so are your other four senses. Your sense of sight is pleased when you look at a beautiful piece of fruit, for instance, and your sense of smell is awakened by the scent of bacon frying. Opening a can of cola and listening to the fizz or chomping on a bag of crisp potato chips involves your sense of hearing. Licking a smooth, cold ice cream cone excites your sense of touch.

There is nothing wrong with enjoying the way food arouses all of your senses. In fact, if you allow yourself to enjoy each bite of food, it is easier to feel satisfied and to know when you have had enough.

Unfortunately, people who suffer from binge eating disorder often don't take time to enjoy their food. They eat because they want to feel differently than they do, much in the way that alcoholics drink because alcohol changes what they feel. Although a person can quit drinking, people who are addicted to food cannot quit eating to solve their problems. As a result, feelings about food become complicated for the binge eater.

An Abundance of Choice

Food is necessary for human life. You need a balanced diet to feed your body and maintain nutritional health. Your ancestors had to grow or kill their own food to survive, and their diets were simple. Sometimes there wasn't enough food. Today, though, you can go to a grocery store or restaurant and probably buy whatever you want to eat. At fast-food restaurants, you can get food without even leaving the car. Restaurants deliver pizza or other food to your home. Food is readily available, plentiful, and convenient, and most people can pick what they want from foods grown and manufactured all over the world.

One of the results of having all these choices is that eating has become an important part of Americans' social life, and many people have developed a love/hate relationship with food. Although the American culture is one obsessed with health and fitness, millions

Drive-through restaurants make buying food at any time of the day or night handy. They also give binge eaters a place to eat alone—in their car—but can lead to distracted and dangerous driving.

of Americans are struggling with what and how much they eat. Their feelings about food have become a national problem.

Weight-Loss Trends

Many binge eaters believe that dieting is the answer to all of their problems. They tell themselves that if they find the right diet and lose weight, all of their problems will disappear and their lives will be perfect. Diets are not a magical cure for the problems faced by binge eaters or anyone else. In fact, dieting can be very dangerous. Binge eaters do not understand what their own bodies need, and diets make the problem worse because dieters must eat according to a strict plan that somebody else has designed for them. These plans usually list "good" and "bad" foods, and they often instruct the dieter to eat much less than his or her body needs to function properly.

Drastically cutting calories can actually sabotage weight loss. When the body suddenly receives fewer calories than it needs, it tries to protect itself from starvation by slowing down the speed at which it burns calories. It also stores extra calories as fat. Furthermore, because dieters force themselves to give up the "bad" foods that they enjoy in exchange for small quantities of "good" foods, it is easy for them to break the diet. Most people who deny their bodies certain foods will eventually go off a diet. When they do "cheat," they often binge eat. While going off a diet is a normal, even healthy, reaction to the restrictions of most diets, binge eaters usually can't forgive themselves for doing it. They see their action as yet another failure.

Even if you've never had an eating disorder, repeated diets can lead you into one. Although between 95 and 98 percent of diets fail, about 25 percent of pathological dieters develop an eating disorder, according to the National Association of Anorexia Nervosa and Associated Disorders. Most teens and tweens should not be on any restrictive diet. Because their bodies are still growing, they need to establish healthy eating habits and should not deprive themselves of essential nutrients. In fact, dieting can lead to weight gain. Teens and tweens worried about their weight should discuss options with their doctors.

Changing Attitudes Toward Food

When you were a very small child, "good" foods were foods you liked and "bad" foods were foods you didn't like. As you got

Easy-to-grab foods such as junk foods, which have little or no nutritional value, are often the foods that binge eaters enjoy eating the most because they believe the snacks will help them feel happy.

older, food began to take on different meanings. You learned these meanings from your parents. As you started to worry about your weight, you learned that "good" foods are low-fat, low-calorie foods such as vegetables, fruits, and grains, and "bad" foods are high-fat/high-calorie foods like sweets, fast foods, and fried snacks or meals. You say that you are "being good" when you eat low-fat/low-calorie foods and "bad" when you eat high-fat/high-calorie foods. For example, a person might say, "I was good today. I only ate a salad." Another might say, "No, I can't have any dinner because I was bad this afternoon. I ate a whole bag of potato chips." Unfortunately, many of the foods that you thought of as good when you were a child are the same foods that you're supposed to think of as bad when you get older.

Food is not good or bad. It's just food! However, people who have problems with food tend to feel that their goodness or badness as human beings is directly related to the food they eat and the size of their bodies. They think that people who eat fattening foods and have large bodies are bad, lazy, and disgusting. In contrast, they think that people who eat low-fat foods and have thin bodies are good, valuable, and attractive. Because most binge eaters enjoy high-fat foods and have large bodies, this way of thinking usually leads to problems of low self-esteem, self-abuse, guilt, and shame.

The Body and Mind

Binge eaters abuse food for many reasons, and all of them have to do with negative self-image. They feel they are not good enough, that nobody could love them as they are, and that they have no self-control. They feel that their fat makes them unworthy of a good life, and they abuse food to avoid dealing directly with their problems. Many studies have linked binge eating with increased anxiety and depression.

Self-Regulation

Babies eat when they are hungry. They cry, and their parents feed them. They will eat as much food as they need and then stop. As children get older, many different factors demand that they eat at certain times. Kids in school are not allowed to eat until the lunch bell rings, and kids at home are not allowed to eat until mealtimes. In addition, many children are told that they must finish all of the food on their plates, whether they are hungry or not. When they finish, they are told that they are good.

Sometimes, adults reward children for good behavior by giving them candy, baking cookies, or taking them out for ice cream. Adults often punish children by making them skip a meal or telling them that they can't have any dessert. As a result, young children begin

Young people who have earned an allowance or work at a part-time job have freedom in deciding what they will eat, especially when they can go out with friends for meals.

to learn at an early age not to trust their own hunger. Somebody else controls what, when, and how much they eat.

When children become teenagers, their parents usually allow them more control over what they eat. Teens sometimes help shop for groceries or prepare dinner. They may have an allowance or a part-time job that allows them to buy snacks or go out to eat with friends. Some buy healthy snacks, but most prefer junk food (food that is high in calories but low in nutrition), particularly if it is forbidden at home.

During this time of greater personal responsibility, teens also find themselves facing at least some of the difficult problems that come with freedom: changing relationships with parents, feelings of loneliness and insecurity, difficulty managing schoolwork and social or extracurricular activities, anxiety about the future, and confusion about sexuality. Teens have different ways of trying to cope with these problems. Some talk to family or friends; others turn to drugs or alcohol. Teens who suffer from binge eating turn to food. It is easier to feel "out of control" about food than it is to feel "out of control" about the problems in your life.

Emotional Eating

Binge eaters try to swallow their emotions by swallowing food. Most of us don't want to experience anger, loneliness, confusion, or fear, but binge eaters attempt to avoid these feelings by focusing all of their emotions around food and weight issues. The unhappiness that comes from overeating, they believe, is easier to deal with than other bad feelings.

Many binge eaters have not experienced enough love in their lives, so they begin to think of food as love. They may have grown up in families where everybody was expected to be an overachiever,

Some young people use eating as a substitute for love. When they are in stressful situations, whether academic or social, they turn to eating to find comfort and relief during their anxious moments.

and they felt pressured to be "perfect." Or their parents and/or brothers and sisters might have been overly critical, always pointing out what was wrong with them and never what was right. In still other instances, family members were not allowed to recognize or express their emotions, particularly feelings of warmth and affection. When people do not have a chance to learn how to have healthy, loving relationships with others, they often turn to a compulsion—in the case of binge eaters, compulsive eating—to fill the emptiness and loneliness in their lives.

Sexuality is one of the toughest issues most teens face. Being sexually attracted to other people is both exciting and scary. Some binge eaters use food abuse and weight gain to protect themselves from feelings that are new and difficult to understand. Weight gain is often an excuse for binge eaters to avoid developing relationships that might lead to sexual feelings and situations.

Binge eaters may also use their weight to avoid other challenges when they're afraid of failure. Instead of participating in activities that will help them meet new people or trying new things that will help them learn about life, they convince themselves that they never had any chance of being successful or accepted because they are fat. They turn to food to calm their fears. Food can't judge them or tell them they aren't good enough.

There are many people who don't like to have confrontations and will do anything to avoid them. Some people feel that they don't have a right to get angry or think they'll lose people in their lives if they get angry at them. Some people deal with their anger by binge eating. But food doesn't and can't make the anger go away. The anger is still there; it's just buried deeper inside.

Biological Basis

Researchers are continuing to look into the biological basis of binge eating disorder. Brain chemicals that regulate appetite and metabolism (how the body uses calories for energy) may play a role. If these parts of the brain do not send the right message to the body when it is full, you may be more likely to binge eat. Additionally, if you have family members affected by binge eating disorder, you are more likely to develop the disorder. This condition indicates a possible genetic connection. Food addiction could also be linked to a genetic mutation.

Some medical research has shown that the size and shape of particular areas of the brain (for example, in the hypothalamus, pituitary gland, and amygdala) are on occasion different in people who have eating disorders. The system involving the hypothalamus, pituitary gland, and amygdala releases some neurotransmitters (the brain's chemical messengers), including serotonin, which help to regulate a person's appetite. An imbalance in serotonin, for example, could account partly for why some people with eating disorders have problems with their need for food.

Physical and Emotional Effects

The physical and emotional toll of binge eating disorder can be immense. Weight gain is the most common effect on the body. This can lead to serious health risks, such as obesity, high blood pressure, diabetes, heart disease, and many others. These may require extensive medical care and monitoring.

Moreover, when eating becomes the central focus of your life, your social and academic activities might begin to suffer as a result. Constantly worrying about what to eat or hiding your eating from your family and friends might mean you begin to withdraw from them. You might find it more challenging to get to school, which could make you feel anxious, stressed, or depressed. Although these effects are serious, you can get help and overcome your disorder.

Physical Effects

Eating a lot of food at once, especially a lot of unhealthy food such as potato chips and cookies, can be very dangerous to your health. Even though you're consuming a lot of calories, they're empty calories and you run the risk of malnutrition. Your body requires a balanced diet and eating in moderation. Overeating can also put you at risk for diseases associated with obesity.

Gaining Weight

Gaining weight is the most obvious sign that you're binge eating. Most people who have this eating disorder are overweight. To try to lose the weight they've gained, many binge eaters get addicted to dieting. They believe diets can help them control their obsession with food. Typically, they become yo-yo dieters, constantly losing and regaining weight in an unhealthy way.

Bingeing and then dieting to lose the weight can lead to a dangerous cycle of weight gain and weight loss. Each time you diet, you may get so hungry that you slip right back into the binge eating cycle.

Weight gain can lead to obesity, a condition that occurs when the body mass index (BMI)—a measure that is based on the ratio of height to weight and is correlated with the amount of body fat—is higher than a certain level. The body mass index is a formula that is frequently used to find out whether a person is underweight, overweight, or about the right weight.

Binge eating can lead to weight gain, and many binge eaters try to lose the extra weight by dieting. However, limiting a diet can often result in more binge eating.

Other Health Risks

Physical health problems binge eaters may experience include high blood pressure, high cholesterol, muscle and joint pain, digestive issues, headaches, and menstrual issues. Gaining excess body weight, whether you are obese or overweight, can also put you at risk for several serious diseases, including:

- High blood pressure
- Type 2 diabetes
- Gallbladder disease

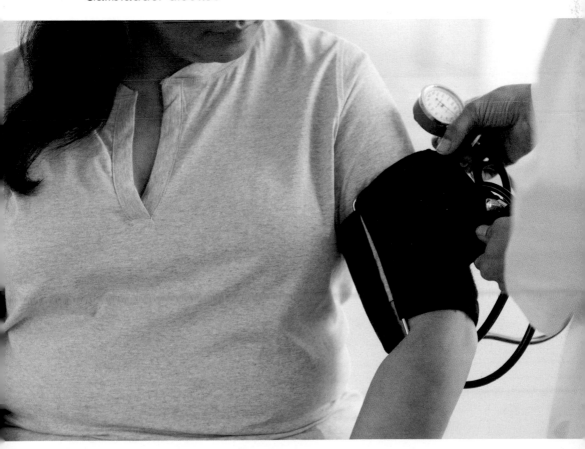

Becoming overweight or obese can lead to having some serious health consequences such as high blood pressure. People with binge eating disorder can be at high risk for getting heart disease.

- Joint problems
- Breathing difficulty
- Heart disease
- Stomach and intestinal problems
- Sleep apnea (when you stop breathing during sleep)
- Certain types of cancer
- Kidney disease
- Liver disease

These issues may require additional medical intervention, and the effects of these problems may further interfere with a binge eater's ability to participate in his or her usual daily activities and social interactions. These may in turn affect his or her emotional well-being.

Emotional Effects

People who are binge eaters are usually very aware that they have a problem. They may feel upset, depressed, and anxious about what they are doing.

Having binge eating disorder may make you go into seclusion. To hide what you're doing, you may stop going to school, visiting friends, and taking part in activities you once loved. And the weight gain that occurs with binge eating can be difficult to bear, especially when other kids make cruel comments.

Research finds that people with eating disorders are more likely to be depressed, stressed, and anxious than those who don't have a disorder. Some studies show that anxiety or depression occurs before the onset of an eating disorder; while in other cases, it accompanies or follows the onset. People who compulsively over-eat are also more likely to commit suicide or have suicidal thoughts.

Frequently binge eaters become disgusted with themselves, embarrassed, and depressed because they overeat and cannot control their bingeing episodes.

No matter how smart, talented, or kind they are, binge eaters feel that their problems with food and weight make them unworthy of the fun, friendship, and happiness that other teens share. They may feel a sense of helplessness because they can't control their eating habits.

Seeking Help

If you think you may be a binge eater, it is important that you look for help. You may feel too ashamed to admit your problem to someone else. Or you may want to keep your overeating a secret, hoping that it will go away on its own. However, please remember that no problem ever disappears if you don't face it honestly. Asking for help is not a sign of weakness. It is a way of showing that you love yourself and are ready to trust others to help you become the best person you can be.

The good news is that binge eating disorder and certain accompanying problems, such as depression and anxiety, can be treated and can often be treated at the same time. Numerous medical and mental health professionals are available to help teens cope with the physical and psychological effects of binge eating.

The first step is to recognize the signs of binge eating disorder. Mental help website helpguide.org recommends asking yourself the following questions:

- Do you feel out of control when you're eating?
- Do you think about food all the time?
- Do you eat in secret?
- Do you eat until you feel sick?
- Do you eat to escape from worries, relieve stress, or to comfort yourself?
- Do you feel disgusted or ashamed after eating?
- Do you feel powerless to stop eating, even though you want to?

The more questions you answer "yes" to, the more likely it is you have a binge eating disorder and need to seek help.

The Road to Recovery

Binge eating disorder requires treatment on both the physical and psychological levels. There is no one course of treatment that fits everyone; rather, patients work with professionals to determine the best options for them. There are many programs and paths to treating binge eating, and it is important to find the one that is right for you. Whatever path is right for you, the sooner you seek help and begin treatment, the better chance you have of overcoming binge eating and the various health problems it might cause.

Seeking Medical Help

The first step in getting treatment for binge eating disorder is to see a doctor. Your doctor is there to help you get better. In order to do that, the doctor will ask you a series of questions. The questions will not only be about your health but also about your feelings about eating, school, and other parts of your life. The questions can help your doctor determine whether you are depressed, angry, or stressed or whether you are having difficulty coping with certain situations in your life. The doctor can also look at some biological factors that can have an effect on bingeing behaviors. It is important to know that some doctors may not be trained to recognize binge eating disorder. If your doctor dismisses your concerns, ask him or her for the name of

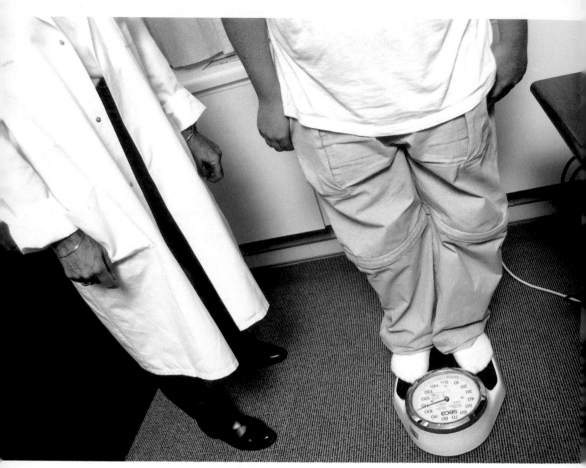

Consult with a doctor about your health. He or she will ask questions about your eating disorder and talk to you about how to incorporate a healthy eating plan and nutrition into your life.

a mental health professional or talk to someone you trust, such as a parent or guidance counselor.

Basic Physical

After asking you some questions, your doctor will examine you to see how healthy you are. He or she will weigh you, measure your height, and calculate your BMI. Then the doctor may check your blood pressure, heart rate, lung function, and other vital signs.

Blood Tests

The doctor may take blood from you to look for the levels of several important substances in your blood, such as cholesterol, blood sugar, and electrolytes. Imbalances of these substances can mean that you have a health problem. Blood tests can also determine whether your thyroid (a gland that produces hormones that control the speed of your body's metabolism) is working properly. Additionally, your doctor will probably look to see whether you have any of the problems associated with binge eating disorder, such as heart disease or sleep apnea.

Checking Psychological Health

Anxiety, depression, and other psychological problems are closely tied to binge eating disorder. Your doctor or a therapist might ask you to fill out questionnaires that ask about your thoughts and feelings and your attitudes about yourself and food. Knowing the answers to these questions can help your doctor design a treatment plan that's right for you, so it's important to be honest. For example, if you're depressed, your doctor may want to put you on antidepressant medications.

Making a Diagnosis

Doctors have certain measurements, called criteria, which they use to diagnose binge eating disorder. These are certain characteristics that people who have this condition share. These are the criteria for binge eating disorder, from the American Psychiatric Association's *Diagnostic and Statistical Manual of Mental Disorders* (DSM):

1) Recurrent and persistent episodes of binge eating
2) Binge eating episodes are associated with three (or more) of the following:
    - Eating much more rapidly than normal
    - Eating until feeling uncomfortably full
    - Eating large amounts of food when not feeling physically hungry
    - Eating alone because of being embarrassed by how much one is eating
    - Feeling disgusted with oneself, depressed, or very guilty after overeating
3) Marked distress regarding binge eating
4) Absence of regular compensatory behaviors (such as purging)

The more detail you can provide about your binge eating episodes, the better equipped your doctor will be to make a diagnosis. Think about such information as how long a specific binge eating episode lasted, how much food you ate, any social or emotional experiences you may have had leading up to the episode, and how you felt before, during, and after.

Finding the Right Treatment

Recovering from an eating disorder is like fighting an addiction to drugs or alcohol. It is a long, slow, and difficult process, and it may never be 100 percent complete. A recovering alcoholic will always have to be careful. Even if she hasn't had a drink in years, she may always have a strong urge to drink. People with eating disorders also have ongoing struggles and may relapse many times. But with treatment, many people do recover and go on to lead happy, fulfilling lives.

The goal for treating this disorder is to stop the bingeing and to get back to a healthy weight. Treatment usually involves seeing a doctor, a dietitian, and a mental health professional such as a psychologist, psychiatrist, or social worker.

Getting Support

As soon as you think you may have a problem with binge eating, try talking to an adult you trust. This person might be a family friend, a parent, or a teacher. If there is something going on in your life that is bothering you or causing you pain, tell that person about it.

Be open to discussing your eating problems with an adult, such as a parent, who is a supportive and dedicated listener.

You may find it easier to accept help from someone you don't know personally. Your school guidance office is a good place to start. Guidance counselors understand the difficulties teens face. Food-related problems have become common among teenagers, and many guidance counselors now know a lot about binge eating. If your guidance counselor can't help you, he or she should be able to direct you to a specialist who can help.

Seeking Counseling

Therapy with a psychologist, psychiatrist, or social worker can help teach you how to come to terms with the emotions that led to your binge eating and help you find healthier ways of coping with those emotions.

One of the most effective treatments for binge eating is called cognitive behavioral therapy. This type of therapy teaches you how to deal with stressful situations, feel better about your body, and eat in a healthier way. Interpersonal therapy is another kind of treatment. It helps you learn how to relate better to your family, friends, and other people in your life. You may also see a dietitian, who can help you relearn your internal hunger signals and establish healthier eating habits. Family therapy can often be very helpful, healing unresolved issues from the past and/or teaching the family healthier ways to function.

Another option is to join a support group where you can meet other teens who share your problems and concerns. Support groups are important because they can help you understand that you are not alone and there are others who have had similar experiences as you.

Find a counselor, therapist, or support group to help you work through your emotional, mental, or self-defeating behaviors so that you can gain control over your eating disorder and discover healthy eating habits.

Medical Treatments

In 2015, Vyvanse, a drug used to treat attention-deficit hyperactivity disorder, was approved for the treatment of binge eating disorder. Questions about its safety are still being considered, but there may be other options for binge eating patients. One type of drug your doctor may prescribe is a type of antidepressant called a selective serotonin reuptake inhibitor (SSRI). This includes Prozac, Paxil, and Zoloft, and they work on a chemical called serotonin, which affects mood and behavior. Studies have shown that SSRIs can relieve depression and help people with binge eating disorder binge less often. If you are depressed, taking antidepressants that have been prescribed by your doctor in addition to the talk therapy portion of your treatment can be very important for your recovery plan. An epilepsy drug called Topamax also helps reduce binge eating behavior and can help people with this disorder lose weight.

Special Programs

Weight-loss programs are run by medical professionals who can show you the best ways to diet and exercise to lose weight. It's best to wait until you are seeking professional help before starting a weight-loss program to ensure your nutritional needs are not neglected. Remember, binge eating is rarely just about food and weight. You have to uncover the deeper reasons behind your binge eating if you want to truly heal.

Reaching Out to a Friend

If you think a friend or family member is a binge eater, talk to him or her about it. Be loving and supportive, and let the person know

Obesity treatment centers offer supportive residential experiences that can help young people lose weight and improve their well-being. They also provide health courses and talks with doctors.

that you are there to help. Share some of the information you have learned about binge eating.

Accepting help or even acknowledging a problem may be difficult for someone at first—don't be surprised or hurt if your friend or loved one does not immediately accept your help or responds with anger or resentment. And don't try to force anyone to accept your help if he or she is resistant. Letting someone know that you are there to listen and care when he or she needs you may eventually encourage your friend to speak more openly or take the first step to seeking care.

10 GREAT QUESIONS TO ASK A DOCTOR OR MEDICAL PROFESSIONAL

Before you go to a doctor or counselor, copy down these questions and bring them with you. They are a good guide to help you start a conversation with the people who will help you recover internally. Some medical professionals may not ask about your eating habits on their own, so being prepared with questions can help initiate your path to recovery.

1. Do I have binge eating disorder?

2. Am I overweight or obese?

3. What effects will binge eating have on my health?

4. What tests will I be given to check my health?

5. How can I control my urge to binge?

6. What treatments are available, and which do you recommend?

7. Are there any side effects I should know about?

8. How will I know if the treatments are effective?

9. How can I maintain a healthy diet and exercise regimen?

10. How do I deal with the emotional issues in my life that led to my binge eating?

CHAPTER FIVE

Changing Your Attitude Toward Food

You have to eat to stay alive, so avoiding food is not an option in the treatment of any eating disorder. However, there are ways to develop a healthy relationship with food. You can rethink how you look at yourself and take concrete steps to help manage your food intake. Changing the way you feel about food can help you improve how you feel about yourself.

Your Self-Esteem

If you are a binge eater, chances are that you are much kinder and more supportive to other people than you are to yourself. You likely suffer from low self-esteem, which means you don't always believe in your own value as a human being. Be aware of when you are being unkind to yourself and work on changing the way you treat yourself. The following are some ways you can begin to change your thinking.

Give Yourself Credit

It's difficult to make your life better tomorrow if you hate who you are today. The next time you find yourself saying or thinking something

Binge eaters usually suffer from a negative body image. Do not criticize yourself or your looks, but instead think about all the beneficial things your body does for you, such as breathing, playing sports, and talking to friends.

unkind about yourself or your body, stop and think whether you would ever say such a mean thing to a family member or a friend. Chances are you wouldn't. You probably don't like to hurt other people's feelings, so why hurt your own?

Try to be more aware of frustrating, self-critical thoughts, and take a moment to apologize to yourself when you hurt yourself. Also try to admire yourself for the good qualities you have that don't revolve around appearance, such as intelligence, generosity, thoughtfulness, kindness, and a sense of humor.

Avoid Comparisons

To the binge eater, other people seem thinner, happier, and more successful. Thin people seem to live easy lives, free of the pain and shame that the binge eater must cope with. However, remember that appearances can be deceiving. All people experience struggles and suffer disappointments—you just can't always see these problems in the people you admire or envy.

Ignore What Others Think and Say

Binge eaters often spend too much time and energy thinking about other people's opinions, real or imagined. They assume the worst, believing that others will reject them or make fun of them because they're overweight. This negative view often prevents them from meeting new friends and participating in fun and interesting activities that they want to try. Some people may treat you badly because of your weight. There will always be unhappy people in the world who feel the need to reject or abuse anyone who is different. But there are people who will like you for who you are.

Looking at Food Differently

In addition to changing your attitude toward others and yourself, you will need to evaluate and change your relationship with food. One of the keys to overcoming binge eating is to learn how to pay closer attention to where, when, what, and how much you are eating.

Your Choice of Food and How You Eat

First, try to avoid dieting. Depriving yourself can make you feel hungrier and restart a pattern of overeating. Also make sure to eat breakfast. Skipping the most important meal of the day will make you hungrier and likely to eat more in the afternoon and evening.

The Department of Agriculture maintains the ChooseMyPlate.gov website, which offers information about nutritious diets that include the five food groups: fruits, vegetables, grains, proteins, and dairy.

Get to know your body. Pay attention to when you are and aren't hungry. If you are craving a sweet snack because you had a rough day, try to hold out until your belly really feels hungry before eating. At mealtimes, try eating slowly while really concentrating on what you're doing. Halfway through the meal, take a break, and ask yourself whether you've had enough. If not, keep eating slowly and carefully. If so, say to yourself, "I've had enough food and I'm finished," and push your plate away.

If you keep eating and finish everything on your plate, take a moment (about ten minutes after you've finished eating) and think about how you feel one last time. Do you feel good or bad? Satisfied or too full? If you feel bad or too full, don't be angry at yourself. Just remember that it takes time to relearn your internal hunger signals, but know that you do have the power to stop eating when you feel satisfied.

Your Eating Location

Try to avoid eating alone in your room or in front of the television. Either of these habits can make you eat more than you normally would. Being distracted by the television or another activity can make you go into automatic mode. You'll lose track of how much you're eating and not realize when you feel full. Instead, try eating at a kitchen or dining room table. Whenever possible, eat with other people. Eating is a natural and pleasurable activity, and you shouldn't feel ashamed or embarrassed about it.

Your Eating Schedule

Binge eaters usually overeat as a reaction to feelings of stress or anxiety. It is important to try to recognize when this is happening and find healthier ways to deal with stressful situations. One way to learn about your own eating patterns is to keep a food diary. In a notebook, write the date and time, list the names and amounts of foods you eat, and write down any thoughts or feelings you had before, during, and after eating. After a while, you will be able to look at your diary and see if there are certain situations or feelings that often cause you to overeat.

Keeping a food diary can teach people about their eating habits, such as the kinds of food they eat, when they eat, how much they eat, and the feelings they have about the food they are consuming.

As you begin to see the patterns in your eating habits, you can look for ways to reduce or replace activities that may cause you stress and drive you to overeat. Your new activities can be as simple as calling a friend to talk or listening to enjoyable music or something more physical, such as relaxation exercises. You'll learn to listen to your body so that you can recognize the difference between your physical need and your emotional need for food. Get strong support from family and friends while you are discovering healthy eating habits. Improving your relationship with food may not come quickly or easily but with the right help, commitment, and tools, you can overcome binge eating disorder and find the right nutritional balance to lead a healthy, rewarding life.

GLOSSARY

ADDICTION A compulsive or obsessive need for and use of a substance.

ANOREXIA NERVOSA An eating disorder in which a person has an intense fear of getting fat, refuses to eat, and keeps losing weight.

ANXIETY A condition marked by a sense of intense uneasiness, dread, or apprehension toward a future or anticipated event or adverse circumstance. The psychological responses are often accompanied by physiological responses, such as sweating or increased pulse.

BINGEING Rapid eating of large amounts of food—2,000 calories or more—during a short period of time.

BODY MASS INDEX (BMI) A measure that relates weight to height. It is the ratio of the body's weight in kilograms to the square of its height in meters.

BULIMIA NERVOSA An eating disorder in which huge amounts of food are eaten, then purged by vomiting, using laxatives, or exercising excessively.

CHOLESTEROL A fatlike substance that comes from foods and is made by the body.

COMPULSION An uncontrollable impulse to do something.

DEPRESSION A medical condition marked by any or all of the following to the point that it prevents normal functioning: extreme sadness, hopelessness, inability to focus and/or act, as well as changes in sleeping and appetite.

ELECTROLYTES Chemicals that are needed for the body to function properly (they affect most metabolic processes).

GENE The basic unit of heredity. Genes code for traits such as hair color and eye color. They are passed down from parents to their children.

GRAZING Eating at different times and places throughout the day.

IDEAL A standard of perfection. In relation to the body, it is often impossible and unhealthy to achieve.

METABOLISM The chemical processes by which the body produces or breaks down substances for energy.

MUTATION A change in the genetic material of a cell.

MYTH An idea or story that many people believe but that is not true.

OBESITY A condition in which the body accumulates and stores excess fat in the body, generally resulting in a body mass index of 30 or higher.

OBSESSION Something you cannot stop thinking or worrying about.

PSYCHOLOGICAL Based in your mind; your thinking and understanding of the events and people in your life.

SELF-ESTEEM The way you see and treat yourself based on your own confidence in and respect for yourself. Also, the feeling that you are someone who deserves to be liked and respected by others.

SENSUAL Appealing to any or all of the five senses: sight, touch, taste, smell, and hearing.

TALK THERAPY A form of counseling or psychotherapy based primarily on discussion and conversation between a patient and therapist.

YO-YO DIETING A habit of losing weight by dieting, followed by regaining weight; often a repeating pattern.

FOR MORE INFORMATION

Binge Eating Disorder Association (BEDA)
637 Emerson Place
Severna Park, MD 21146
(855) 855-2332
Website: http://bedaonline.com
BEDA works to expand awareness about binge eating disorder
and provides resources and hope to those affected by it.
The organization is also engaged in various outreach activities to effect change in education and government policy.

The Eating Disorder Foundation
1901 East 20th Avenue
Denver, CO 80205
(303) 322-3373
Website: http://www.eatingdisorderfoundation.org
The Eating Disorder Foundation is active in education and
advocacy initiatives targeting the prevention and elimination
of eating disorders. The organization works with schools,
medical centers, and fitness centers to develop programs
that target the needs of various age groups.

Hopewell
404 McArthur Avenue
Ottawa, ON K1K 1G8
Canada
(613) 241-3428
Website: http://www.hopewell.ca
Hopewell is dedicated to supporting those affected by eating
disorders and works to support prevention by encouraging

healthy lifestyles and attitudes. Various resources are available for individuals, families, professionals, and more.

National Association of Anorexia Nervosa and Associated
    Eating Disorders (ANAD)
750 E. Diehl Road, #127
Naperville, IL 60563
(630) 577-1330
Website: http://www.anad.org
ANAD works to increase awareness of various eating disorders,
    including anorexia nervosa, bulimia nervosa, and binge
    eating disorder. It supports education, prevention, and
    recovery efforts for families and professionals through
    research and other services.

The National Association for Males with Eating Disorders
    (NAMED)
164 Palm Drive, #2
Naples, FL 34112
Website: http://namedinc.org
As the only organization in the United States dedicated exclu-
    sively to supporting men and boys with an eating disorder,
    NAMED seeks to fill the gap in resources and support for a
    population typically underrepresented In research and out-
    reach efforts.

National Eating Disorder Information Centre (NEDIC)
ES 7-421, 200 Elizabeth Street
Toronto, ON M5G 2C4
Canada

(416) 340-4156

Website: http://www.nedic.ca

NEDIC offers outreach, education, and direct client support to
Canadians suffering from or seeking more information on
various eating disorders. Callers can also contact its toll-free
hotline (866-633-4220) to get information about treatment
and support options.

National Eating Disorders Association (NEDA)

165 West 46th Street, Suite 402

New York, NY 10036

(212) 575-6200

Website: http://www.nationaleatingdisorders.org

NEDA helps to encourage people who are affected by eating
disorders, including binge eating disorder. It offers an inter-
active website for teens Proud2Bme.org, a safe community
for young people to discuss their concerns.

Overeaters Anonymous

6075 Zenith Court NE

Rio Rancho, NM 87144

(505) 891-2664

Website: https://www.oa.org

Overeaters Anonymous is a fellowship of individuals dedicated
to supporting each other through the process of dealing
with binge eating, obesity, and various other behaviors
related to food using the organization's twelve-step process.
Meetings are held throughout the country, are free to attend-
ees, and offer unconditional support and acceptance.

US Department of Agriculture (USDA)
Center for Nutrition Policy and Promotion
3101 Park Center Drive
Alexandria, VA 22302-1594
Website: http://www.choosemyplate.gov
The USDA ChooseMyPlate website provides information about
    nutrition and healthy diets. It offers online sources for plan-
    ning and preparing meals, menu suggestions, nutrition plans
    and trackers, and building a cookbook.

Websites
Because of the changing nature of Internet links, Rosen
    Publishing has developed an online list of websites related
    to the subject of this book. This site is updated regularly.
    Please use this link to access this list:

http://www.rosenlinks.com/CED/Binge

FOR FURTHER READING

Ambrose, Marylou, and Veronica Deisler. *Investigating Eating Disorders (Anorexia, Bulimia, and Binge Eating): Real Facts for Real Lives*. Berkeley Heights, NJ: Enslow Publishers, 2011.

Barbour, Scott. *Obesity* (Opposing Viewpoints). Detroit, MI: Greenhaven Press, 2010.

Haugen, David M., ed. *Nutrition* (Opposing Viewpoints). Detroit, MI: Greenhaven Press, 2011.

Laser, Tammy, and Stephanie Watson. *Eating Disorders*. New York, NY: Rosen Publishing, 2012.

Levete, Sarah. *The Hidden Story of Eating Disorders*. New York, NY: Rosen Publishing, 2014.

Lew, Kristi. *I Have an Eating Disorder. Now What?* New York, NY: Rosen Publishing, 2015.

Marisco, Katie. *Eating Disorders*. New York, NY: Cavendish Square Publishing, 2014.

Murphy, Wendy B. *Obesity*. Minneapolis, MN: Twenty-First Century Books, 2012.

Smith, Rita, Vanessa Baish, Edward Willett, and Stephanie Watson. *Self-Image and Eating Disorders*. New York, NY: Rosen Publishing, 2013.

Smolin, Lori A., and Mary B. Grosvenor. *Nutrition and Eating Disorders*. New York, NY: Chelsea House, 2011.

Smolin, Lori A., and Mary B. Grosvenor. *Nutrition and Weight Management*. New York, NY: Chelsea House, 2010.

Watson, Stephanie. *Frequently Asked Questions About Weight Loss*. New York, NY: Rosen Publishing, 2013.

Zoumbaris, Sharon K. *Nutrition*. Santa Barbara, CA: ABC-CLIO, 2009.

About the Authors

Nita Mallick is a writer based in central New Jersey. She majored in psychology in college where she performed research on various social and cultural issues.

Stephanie Watson is an award-winning writer based in Rhode Island. She is a regular contributor to several online and print publications, and she has written or contributed to more than two dozen books.

Photo credits

Cover, p.3 © iStockphoto.com/KatarzynaBialasiewicz; p. 6 © Nadezhda Bolotina/Shutterstock.com; p. 8 Robert E Daemmrich/The Image Bank/Getty Images; p. 9 Brian Goodman/Shutterstock.com; p. 13 Photographee.eu/Shutterstock.com; p. 15 Peter Dazeley/Photographer's Choice/Getty Images; p. 19 Paolo Bona/Shutterstock.com; p. 22 Ministr-84/Shutterstock.com; p. 24 runzelkorn/Shutterstock.com; p. 26 White Packert/The Image Bank/Getty Images; p. 28 © Shotshop GmbH/Alamy; p. 32 EdBockStock/Shutterstock.com; p. 33 Tetra Images/SuperStock; p. 35 © iStockphoto.com/t-lorien; p. 38 © BSIP SA/Alamy; p. 41 © iStockphoto.com/digitalskillet; p. 43 Tetra Images/Getty Images; p. 45 AJPhoto/Hôpital de Pédiatrie et de Rééducation de Bullion/Science Source; p. 48 © iStockphoto.com/cjmkendry; p. 50 © iStockphoto.com/YinYang; p. 52 © iStocphoto.com/rez-art

Photo Researcher: Nicole DiMella